Designed by Robert Drummond

Cover art by April Vollmer
        "Inhale #1," 2011, 19 x 26 inches
        Digital print and silkscreen on handmade
        Japanese paper

Author photo by Scott Baxter

Published by Barrow Street Press
Distributed by:
        Barrow Street Books
        P.O. Box 1558
        Kingston, RI 02881

First Edition

Library of Congress Control Number: 2012922300

ISBN 978-0-9819876-8-2

CONTENTS

and if it be not broken, break

I

No Threat, Nuthatch

Tiny presence in the pines,
hold still. Upside down—
right side up—flock of nerves
and fretful hunger. Hold still.

Your brothers and your sisters
have forgotten me. That's how still
I have managed to be,
pip pip pip. No stillness
for the foragers. How I love
to make no difference here.

My throat like yours—
rapid little tremor,
heart-freight, air.

Gray Area

(waiting for transplant)

After the call that went nowhere—
though it led him into the cold garage
(alarming chill, halting breath),

over the elegant bridge (the beauty of the night,
and the bridge itself, fused with the burgeoning fear,
We're here, we're here), into the fluorescent

airless hospital (paperwork, forms, drips)
and then out of the surgical garments,
woozy with Atavan, back to the same house,

in his same form—after all that, he said,
just as we started to hang up:
The thing about it . . . I kept thinking

that's the last time I'll use that machine (stair chair)
the last time I'll use that *machine (oxygen compressor)*
the last time   the last time

for each act that causes a crisis of air,
chaos of not enough, *last time* for each tool
that imposes distance between crises—

Though it wasn't. False alarm.
Still, the general notion holds: one night soon
he'll never have those lungs again.

~

Days later, I asked my mother
how it was, when the call came.
She asked if I remembered the August night

the neighbor's house burned down—
smoke billowing, Dad worried for the air,
his house. So they arrived.

He wore the loose green cap, hospital gown, began
those dripping meds. Then, at six or so,
at dawn, No, no match. *Come on then, home.*

Wreck Me

The context has dissolved: I've lost
what I saw first, must have seen,
the car before it flung
itself across the lanes—
I've also lost the sound.
I can see the sidewise vehicle
blue against the nighttime freeway sky,
suspended like the panel of a comic.
Sparks float and melt in the dark,
shreds of oblivion, deflating,
beautiful and almost
simultaneously wretched.
And gone, and my body
calling already for the memory,
wanting the image back:
lovely, appalling. Awful
right there.

~

M reports: the fear of death
is always at us, bossing our fatal
choices. Or this is what I hear

of what he says, gripped
in fear of the smaller death
we'd have to live on after.

~

Why do I choose the same hike
again and again? I want to say,
To see more.
Is it just the opposite?

    ~

I burned the things I wrote.
The fire made such sounds.

Warm at my back, and also when I turned
to blanch my face.

    ~

The car lifts as if driving
across a helix, but the road
won't hold, the cement
doesn't flex or twist
like a ribbon, swift path
to illumination. Sparks—
they swell initially.

I saw it sail.
*There was another
world.* The soundless car
was proof. Such certainties
evaporate in the chest:

my first thought
was promise, but for
that other person,
all the fire burned
once he was over.

~

I (who would usually
obey Park Service Regulations
to the letter) have skittered
off the trail, almost at a run,
trying to keep a footing and skirt
the protruding rust-red outcrop
—sacred vortex!—but I can't
get far enough away not to hear
the woman on her cell,
Yeah, there's good reception here . . .
she's not shouting, but now I know
what her kids watched last night,
and how she saw a *bevy of javelinas,*
she wants to *share this stunning landscape,*
she wants she wants—

M says no one speaks to another
but through his own wants. We read
the lives of others this way: it's why
we should not give advice, wise counsel,
and she keeps almost concluding,
then going on, talking and descending now.
So proud, she says, of something.

Celtic tarot:
             One card spills
as I shuffle the deck,
preparing to choose
some solution to be given. My clairvoyant
says, with real heat,
Let's have *that* one then—

                    Card of Presence.

I am in you and you are in me.

No comma, no subordination.

She says nothing. She says add
another.

Heartland of trust, it reads.

The shimmering horse kneels
to drink the shimmering water.

Drive me away

Drive me home

Open your mouth

I have something

for you

I am going

I'll be back

Eat   Look

Your hand belongs

on my belly

Even harder

I'm still yours

still need you

to lean toward

to see me

to heal   keep me

attached to the surface

of the mountainous world

~

The birds are eating insects they stored
in the bark months ago.

Lucky us: cars in the lot,
all the restaurants open.

~

When we saw the accident
(though I keep thinking
that's the wrong noun,
evasive—what are the real
odds of fluke malfunction?)
there were five of us
together, en route home
from a dinner, a birthday
celebration. There was that instant
of confirmation, *what we saw.*

Then I was the one dialing,
and the operator, dismissive,
already knew. *South of Shea? Yes.*
A dutiful sorority
all calling within seconds
of what must have been the death—

Someone extinguished,
the air   suffused with what?

Lingering nuclei of "presence"?

Today I see, in Recent Calls,
between icons for my friends
at home, at work, my own
number, too, and then *Emergency.*

The driver . . . always
a sucker for the drama?
Or just—that night—decisive, quick?

~

My second fire burned much better
than my first. The first one
needed pages as kindling,
and it faltered anyway.
This second fire's a perfect
picture-postcard fire. Congregation
of ordinary flames. Still,
I see beneath it the silty
ashes, downy remnants
of what I had to purge
—shifting as if a breath
were drawing through them,
trick of the flue.

~

M finds old letters, prehistory,
that to him suggest substrata
of estrangement:

must be insurmountable,
if the evidence goes back.

Oh his will.

The world full of signs
and patterns to decode,
interpret. Zodiac
of will. Does it matter he embraces

his own designation: *cusp*. His moon?
The bull-and-twins. The scale.

Is it time to relinquish
everything, ours a life to study
not inhabit anymore?

When he mounts his case, my blood
goes thick and still. Pressure
in the rib cage, glacial clench.

He owns my body? No. He's in my bloodstream

and constricting—

I burned my hand, collecting
a loaf pan from the oven rack.
Half moon of puffed brown paper.
Underneath, interior, the raw pink
willingness to heal.
Which must be hidden—

Protect us from the avid sun.

I mean each one.

I mean us both.

COLD

(Chronic Obstructive Lung Disease)

What you feel is no air making it in,
I ran out of air, my father always says,
recovering, *just flat out ran out of air.*

But in fact the faltering lungs do not
expel it. *Air remains trapped
in the overinflated lungs.*

All those pulsing sacs and satchels,
beat to hell, unable to deflate.
The little trading floor

of the lungs imbalanced, shutting down.
When it seizes, peaks, when there's
no air: how quickly the skin

and yes the nether-heart go cold,
cold as the grave, sure,
the earthly shoulder turning.

For Doctor Joshua Sonett

Like the hood of a car, he'd said,
referring to the chest
of my father, where he planned
in a year or so to break ribs
and fold open the cracked vessel
unconscious there, a station wagon
of a man on the table, long, long and
a lot like a station wagon but not
new plugs, new lungs.
The warm grayed withered ones
dropped in a bucket, a *pan.*
The body that caused my body to be,
the body split to be made strong,
the body inside which his hands—

'Tis Often Thus with Spirits

Not cognac, though possibly cognac
helps us see them stirring—

the numinous little ghostlings
sloughing off their stardust

in the open field, at night, away from life
and all its fretful particles.

Ghosts like the open land.
They keep their distance.

Often of course suggests they also
come up closer anyway.

She sees them, my little girl,
she sleeps with her eyes open

so they won't come in the window.
That works because they have no wish

to occupy a quiet sleeper, no,
not that. And no messages, no

gluttonous predatory kicks:
they get out there in the open

field, the wilder part of any place,
and *move in their own beauteous forms*

attired, but then sometimes
they want an audience.

They know she loves and fears and loves
sublimity. Here one comes,

into the courtyard—made of light, a fierce
tight glittering. Presence made of nothing

but presence. We love
that ravishment; we trust it.

Science of the Real

Geology, for example—the way the clinker baked
into existence as coal burned underground,
ignited by a bolt of lightning:
a volley from way high in the heavens
transmuted stuff below the crust.

Or: the history of blood transfusion.
Poor Pope Innocent in 1492,
who had to drink some, who then died,
as did the donors.
Or that poor dog Newton watched
transfused but unanesthetized—
he also died.

Hollow goose quills,
hollow metal tubes
and tubes of silver.

My baby had one: i.v. tucked into his scalp.

I watched the torpid liquid seem as if
it wasn't seeping into him.
His skin more wan, or more translucent?
I don't know. He was inert,
exhausted, in a nest of tubes and wires.

I read a novel set in Istanbul.
There was a second bag.

They said it worked. He never
crossed the line. Though I suspect
that line is only real
in terms that aren't sufficient to a mother.

He'd been hemorrhaging, they guessed,
in utero, and undetectably.
His blood loose in me

not so different from Innocent's,
or Innocent's concoction, sloshing
in the wrong organ. All wrong, but lucky us:

we filled his veins and ventricles.
He is the happiest and most robust. No promises,
said the monitors, they only ticked
and glimmered while we watched, transfixed.

The Secret Mind, the Silken Nerve

He has stars in his hair,
yellow head ashine while the moon
tousles through the window.

His breath labors in his lungs
the size of fruits; they press
out each trochee of his dream,

and then a little cough.
The fever's down. On TV
there is a war, two wars.

The whole world
rings in at two-thirds
what it's worth, or used to be,

or less. Just like the walls—
His face twitches
with whatever story

the moon shushes in his ear;
he winces, then he sighs. Why bother
to stand guard, dreaming up

celestial tenderness? He's too big
for any spaces in my body. My mind
sends up a line, *Be faithful   Go*

Even from here, I think.
This bedside.
You should go.

II

People of New York

I know you are dying
as always, even you big ones
from Queens, or from Nyack,
and I'm in the habit
of checking the clock,
midnight again. Again no
phone call, no lungs
expanding and contracting
with some machine
for a brain while the hospital
empties and a family consents
and either in person or over the phone
offers up the life left
in the life that is leaving them.

My father asleep in his bed.

People of New York
New Jersey Connecticut:
I was born there, and he was,
and we lived there and married
and drove to the sea.

They can come from as far
as South Carolina; the doctors
say motorcycle season
is often a good time of year.

Thank you, you bikers.
                    Be careful, be
careful—

We're eighteen months into
the eighteen-month window.
They're dying, I know it,
B+ tall guys

whose lungs vanish
into a furnace, into the ground.

People of New York:
I wish you long lives.
I have no sense of coming
before you, but I know
you are dying as always.
Can you please check the box—
through the DMV,
through the registries?
Have you said, Make me useful,
if the time comes? Dear?

Monsoon

I wanted the storm to hit—surely more
than I wanted the previous weather,
          a dense, numbing kind of pressure.

I must have wanted the strike of it.

Clean sky after:

so utterly open one gets dizzy looking out,
          falling away from the world,
               away and away into that blank.

We wanted the storm? or required it—?

But needing to be harrowed
and being harrowed—

                    even when you provoke it somehow,
                    or vault there,

it's not as you've imagined, not what I

imagined. I can't deliver it: the name
of the storm I always register
as a French pronoun, *mine*
                    mon

my swoon?
my imminent what?

And even having craved the storm,

          (coward need)

even having opened to its electric violence

(no hiding in the archway,
   duct tape across the windows)

I must have had in mind *ensuing calm.*

And now the sky's completely different, indifferent.

But clear.

A morning, our morning,
stars held back behind the light.

In Love's Soft Surgery Skill'd

The body I know best belongs to you

We know each other's best
as if escape—or vicarious
dominion—were the net result
of many years of love

Your body aching yesterday

each muscle calling out
its reverie of pain   I knew
what not to do

And if you turned to me
(you would be wanting to *bestow*
          you never seek much comfort

          afraid, I wonder, of *that* vein
all depth and switchback)

you'd turn with such precise attention

I reply to almost nothing
which   (I know this too)
provides a reason not to reach

Suture

They say the lips
of the wound need
stitching together.

So much can go wrong
at the site. Silence or join
anything and wonder

whether it takes.
Ravenous fusion,
indifferent bacilli.

Dear Matthew

So: He had in mind to divorce her quietly. (1:19)

> She had in mind NewsChannel Four,
> hyperbole laced with facts, best
> damnation by what's not said.
>
> Or she had in mind to reconcile,
> to be permitted again the kindness
> of desire, permission yes to see him welcome
> love, his mouth soft.
>
> Or years of resentment, small bickerings,
> small joys, small bitter coagulants
> lacily, icily adhering
> to the edges of the livable.
>
> > An angel intervened.

And having been cautioned in a dream not to go back to Herod, they returned to their country by another route. (2:12)

> The king, murderous. The wise men, wise,
>
> who returned by an unexpected path.
>
> My country, sweet land,
> interior.
>
> Threat level?

How could we arrive home
in a new way?

I've been warned. Home may be a desert
or a desert lake.

~

Produce fruit in keeping with repentance. (3:8)

Tulip of forgiveness,
melon of peace.

It is a form of obedience, this basket.

I obey, even if you don't eat.

~

Stay salty. Let your light shine. (5:13-14)

The light of salt is like the light of gemstones,
faceted.

Though commonplace, and savory.

Salt: intensifies, provokes, tenderizes.

Your wounds, your dinner.

How can I be light and salt?

Our tears   Our eyes

~

Anger amounts to murder: so reconcile,
then come to the altar with your gift. (5:15-24)

      Vascular, this poison of our anger.

      We could treat it with raw steak,
      flesh of some other,

                as for a wincing eye.

      Or apply a cantaloupe's
                      cool warren of seed.

      In which case, grill the steaks,
      then set the crystal vase and the silverware
                outside, on the terrace, at the mosaic table.

~

The eye is the lamp of the body. (6:22)

      No blood for oil, but blood *as*
      oil. Liquid blue and red

like states of mind,
or of the union.

Blood runs blue in the vessel,
goes red in the air: steady and dark

in safer channels but rancorous
exposed: fuel, the movement of fuel—

delivery to every pore.

My body the globe
                around this light.

Or is it the compound
                from which light can emerge?

And so my eye signals
                presence: the place may be warm,
                there may be dinner there,
                there may be someone saying grace.

Lamplight means a tended fire, after all.

Who of you by worrying can add a single hour to his life? (6:27)

        How did this question last
        through all the vetting and revisions?

        Christ critiques the verb more than its object:
                worrying, which means longing, and intending.

Instead it's

Yield yourselves. Be melons.

Don't think: *extend, control,*

think: *expand;*
                think *yield.*
                        As in give way,

also harvest. Lemons, felons.

Relinquish and generate—relinquish in order to generate.

I fell in love with a maker and he died.

Seemed to die.

                The angel says I don't know how to "die

into"—

                —someone's arms? glacial change? the new?
                myself?

You may not want me to be yours.

But how can you be rid of me?

Lilies into the fire? You can eat them.

Tiger, stargazer: powder stain at the corner of my lip.

~

But go and learn what this means: I desire mercy, not sacrifice. (9:13)

And three chapters later, again. Mercy, not sacrifice. (12:7)

> The lesson bore repeating, reveals
> what gods desire
> and persons lack an instinct for.
>
> As when:
>
> one partner discovers a betrayal. Mercy
> we don't feel with ease but understand:
> we know compassion fuels
> the laying down of arms.
>
> But which *sacrifice* must be renounced?
>
> > The one where someone is thrown over, flayed?
> > > (Yet mercy includes that relinquishment
> > > already, right?)
> >
> > Does he mean no sacrifice in which someone
> > who's been betrayed invites additional mistreatment?
> >
> > > Mercy, we are meant to learn,
> > > does not call for self-eradication—
> >
> > elusive cusp of mercy where we love chit-free.

Every kingdom divided against itself will be ruined, and every city or household divided against itself will not stand. (12:25)

> Dear Matthew, you offer not knowledge but soap,
> to cleanse all manner of lacerations,
> that we may see them, that they not suppurate.
>
> Why make Christ human
> if not to force our search for answers
> into ourselves.
>
> Answers, and acts,
>
>   i.e., mercy, not pity.
>
> Not rage, not self-delusion. *Mercy.*
>
> The most honest human choice,
>
> since we are all the same,
> and since we all want to be *better than.* We choke
> on what we think we deserve.
>
> Mercy honeydew, ice green
> that shines beneath the thickened rind—
> make a poultice of the liquid flesh
> and share it wherever there is harm.

High Desert

Ocotillo, juniper, prickly pear: how staunch
these life-bound clingers-to-the-rocks.
They're almost dead, or so they seem
with their twisting arthritic fingers,
the prickly pear a hunched cluster
of hostility and fruit.

The trees: *junipers,* my birth month
tucked inside their name, they look
like someone stripped their flesh away,
all ragged sinew, contortionists
with open arms.

This one has a bicep, he's a show-off
making muscles in the sun. Existence
a static grudge, while others
on the south face curve and reach
like Martha Graham, elegant,
so open. They give themselves,
they trust the air. Afraid of—
not punishment, and not caress.

That Inner Cavern

Dear Mom, How'd it go with Ed and Helen?
Did you actually discuss Mr. New-Lungs-
Off-to-New-Zealand? Maybe it was enough
just being at the table, that guy a silent fifth:
you four all telling stories, case histories of the recipes,
the night you went to Chinatown, the shifts
of fortune for the plumbing industry. . . . What needs
saying often ends up said by accident
or surreptitiously, when talk is easy,
commonplace. Casualty of our never
being casual together. I wish you could tell me
things like that, offhand. As if it were
still summertime, and we were making dinner.
Summer, when daughters mean *descent, relief.*

In Context

Other problems: heart condition,
atrial fibrillation, flutter of not doing
the damn job. Hole in the leg, his calf,
surgery a good idea but not for him—
too risky. Hole in his leg, heart on the fritz,
lungs plunging inadequate so we sift
the air for him, deliver it pure, O_2—
pumped right into the nostrils.

What is happening in his jaw?
The clench, or the unclench,
the rage-grip, or an easing:
*Here I am, here are my hopes,
my thanks. I'm running
a business, I'm at my desk.*

Parable

Between the path and someone's wall, most likely upside down, the
        chollas scatter.
I'm white, and walking Cosmo. The sharp bulbs cluster almost
        self-contained.
The road startles my attention back with a swooping-in of laughter:

silent electric minibike, weird stealth and sudden chatter,
two riders, girls in ponytails—they're also white, their minibike careens.
The girls, pre-teen, whoosh near; I flinch and smile, scattered,

disrupted mid-cactus-reverie, tall lady in green sneakers staring after—
"Hey nigger!" She shouted this, at me. What did she mean?
A lark, a joke, suburban insularity? Her cold lean peal of angry laughter

lingers in the empty road, a presence in the air like shifting weather.
How strange. So many questions rise and multiply and intersect between
those girls and me. They really yelled that? Merely naughty now? Each
        scatters.

Did what she said have *anything* to do with race? Or was it just intent-to-
        shatter
what I'd presume, expect, of them? I'm curious, and feel the serpentine
undoing of a need—to be myself, to not be anyone. My flustered laughter

fails and leaves a residue of grief, another worry, another thing the matter.
The imaginary money's disappeared, and now the harmony, the sheen
of peace. The girls test meanness knowing it will scatter?
—dissipate into the desert air, confident and flown, like laughter.

Quarry

After a day of hopelessness about our possible
return to forging on, I dreamt a field of tiny pillars.
The field was neat, almost a fairway.
I saw the pillars were owls
standing at intervals, spotting the field,
downy gray, those geometric eyes.
I approached the nearest one,
my heart stirring with gratitude,
a sudden rush of optimistic eagerness.
My nature, I've been told, hope and hunger joined.

I stepped in range of where I could reach out
to touch the bird. There was no contact.
Then it fell, gently forward to one side,
and rolled, long dead, and as I took
the forward step I took before recoiling,
its eyes and beak fell out, dislodged: the whole center
of its desiccated face and brain.

What do birds mean, in dreams?
What wisdom failed or died?
What flight, what predatory urge?

III

Butterfly Wing in Brazil, Etc.

for Celia

Today I walked by the river and watched
large birds—on downdrafts? thermals?—
coast so long across the sky
they seemed not flesh and bone and beak
but only will, pitched into the restless air.

Cresting an easy hill, I found three does,
and after long stares, they ran and leapt and *ran
away*, white flags of sayonara flickering
as they ran and ran and ran
                              so far I thought,

I'm still the cause of *that*—and then, specks,
they disappeared. So when your father said
you came to him and asked to see
my picture, I thought: I caused the deer
some exercise, small racing of the heart.
After a certain point, they were just running.

But now I'm looking at your picture, distant
daughter: my bird of prey, my satchelful
of longing. We can go on
past all going—dream of me, I'm almost there.

I Saw Him Silhouetted at Sundown, in That Light He Was Gray

The white horse is not exactly white,
though his overall effect is whiteness of horse,
white disruption in the silvery field.

His muzzle, charcoal,
his forelock about the color
of my own dirty-blonde hair.

Large veins lift against
the whiteness of his soft cheek.
His blood moves full of messages—

he is a system of synapses
and pulleys and generally so like us
with our ligaments, rippling, healing,

our slightest movements, all the electrons
in sync. . . . He is a deep looker,
a soft white bulletin about attention.

Or inwardness. He sees through me, as you do.
He withstands the enormous pressure
of the wind and sky, of being seen.

Love Poem in December

The river was frozen, now half of it
unclenches—the liquid river frolics
against the floe of ice remaining,
rippling its insistent sexual song.
The grasses are dormant,
shaped like the absent bodies
of the deer who sleep here,
who sip from this cold cup
before they sleep the light sleep
of deer.
        Into these cushioning
grasses I kneel, I settle, to listen
to the water—
               but the suffering ice
rumbles, it intrudes really,
on the cunnilingual passage of the other water—
the water that runs, whispers,
teasing water of false spring.

Visiting the Real Ranch

for Oscar

Here there are places remarkable
for how no one ever comes—no asphalt,
no people, no trivia:

only hills, creeks, cattle.

Some irritating prairie dogs protected
by environmental urgency,
who are interesting,
comic, even as they
wreck the place.

I hope you get to live somewhere like this,
so much yourself you could take charge
of such a solid stand of hills,
receive this evening light, keen and fleeting.

At every moment the valley brimming,
the valley empty.

—Though you are nearly always happy,
and this place is not.

Happiness is for—?

Today, it's my one wish.

Oh, you're such a ham, who would you amuse—

the horse, the white horse on his hill?

Eight-to-Twelve-Hour Surgery

Bucking bronchus, honky-tonkus
Alveoli a viola olive avarice
anastomosis and the blue tubule
The bronchioles and orioles and aureoles
Milk and honey, my milk money
venous *trimmed back*, gloved hand
Venus de Milo à la Sandro, Venus
on the half shell, plasticity
you like those cold and slippery
wet pinky-gray shellfish, throbbing
responsive like a chest cavity—No more,
old man, no more—Pulmonary Venus—
O vertiginous, O vexatious
Suture him suture him suture him home

Tributary

About the sea we love the combination
comfort and menace, the sense of water
gently holding us, of depths engulfing—

we love to be the smallest particle,
germinal, relieved of any prowess
or conviction about prowess,

about control. Inside the sea I know
I love the salty shoring up; I love
the way a wave will take my body

and cleave the foam with me
as with a post. My almost
running out of air. And in your room,

up those many flights
above the Hudson, you can see the river
when you're strong enough to stand.

You stand, your hands
on the metal walker, and you see
the strand of water held so gingerly

between the leafy banks, and there,
to see the many-masted sailing ships
gives your emaciated

muscle an inclination, synaptic *yes*
of movement toward whatever
your heart skips toward.

Walk, you. Walk now,
so you can come
and swim with me.

Plate Tectonics

A suture zone is where a giant
mountain range emerges:
Rockies, Alps, Sierra Madres,
the great plates ground together
and held fast. *Cheyenne belt suture zone,*
the closest one to where I live,
closest of those scars.

Ice, joy. Proximity to heaven,
the heaven of fixed stars—
Let us turn our eyes
to the beautiful eyes.
I am a Gemini: those twins.
Fusion, concatenation—atomically
aortically—the magma and the clouds,
the flesh and also psyche,
I'm not aiming to contain,
$\qquad\qquad\qquad\qquad$ but go there, yes.

Past All Accident

Will / Fate / Chance
—three heads, three tails
swallowed in one knot: ouroboros
of responsibility. I'm not sure
what my interest even yields. . . .

For example, why does anything happen?
The *why* accounts for what percent
of our reply? And which aspects
of the why—aren't some in you
and some in me? Aren't they nearly infinite?

What matters about pain
is how it feels, you said. As if the thicket
of its sources in which we've lost ourselves
won't teach us anything—

what we find here
must cut us but also doesn't matter?
Sometimes I fear I've been
a baby or a hypocrite:
all pout, or all projection.

It's the "all" in Williams that confounds me;
we love each other because we will it so.
Yes, of course. But past all accident?
Accident is everywhere
and yet the doctor means *beyond* it.
Not a victory of will, some deeper helplessness.

The Great Beyonder, said that psychic
after showing me the horse.

Why not come with me?

Flash

The field is full of fifty deer.
They have cliques, it looks like;
some have antlers. Their white tails
seem brighter in the dusk.

They watch as I come around
the elbow of the road. Such
an audience, each face a rigid
signature of attention. I want to give

the deer the news. They will not die
miserably for lack of what is found here.
Really, I have news my   —but when
I make as if to speak, they flee.

Fancy

I might someday become a birder.
I do have that competitive gene, and I love to see
the Barnegat ospreys, redwings, bobtails,
and here even the ho-hum cactus wren.

I used to have a bird: Sydney, gentle affectionate
parakeet. He perched on the ceiling pipes;
he tangled in my hair at nape and ear. Little Sydney—
cheerful hops, friction of his hell-bent wings.

A medievalist once told me a bird is always
what pistols always are, symbolically, in later periods,
and I believe this. Sydney liked to rub his head
against my eyes, and I love to do this with you,

my bird in the hand, my love, my flight.

Sky Islands

Eastern border between states,
southern border between nations:
the Chiricahuas. We're in the corner
astronomers say is darkest in America,
and the sky at night says yes.
Says, You want stars?
I'll smear them in your nose and eyes.
And they are near and far, Venus huge
and then the constellations
all awash in smaller glitter. Mars.

Sometimes I am Orion, armed
and tall and potent. Sometimes I'm a speck
of utter nothing. The dark at first domain,
then later depthless, obliterating.

Borders . . . at the edge,
the sky says, You have no idea.
You think you know me
but you have no hope of knowing.

Inside Arizona, Border Patrol:
big white trucks with gold medallions,
every mile a "presence," U.S. flex.
Off duty, one of these guys runs us
off the road—

Lucky not to have flipped, lucky
to drive on, but not until after confrontation:
his shirt yanked up to show the sidearm, sad-sack story
(agent en route to visit injured child in hospital)
and we're all fine, the car
is probably fine—but the edge
has chasmed there again. So near.

Straddle of shoulder
and gravel ditch, your hands
holding the wheel: hands of force
and tenderness. Riding out the scare,
those hands I trust to have
and hold me, to bring my life alive
inside the shell of me.

That night you tell the story, play guitar.
Music from your fingertips.

In the morning I look out, look south, to Mexico.
The flats—this *sea of grasses*—and then the rising hills,
countless destinations, fluid the way
the galaxies were fluid in the dark.

Here we are. We've brought the center
to the edge.

I wake you with my hands.

Notes

The epigraph is from William Cowper's *Olney Hymns*.

"'*Tis Often Thus with Spirits*": Section XL, *Zóphiël: or the Bride of Seven*, Maria Gowen Brooks, (London: RJ Kennett, 1833).

"Science of the Real": "The Poet," *Essays: second series*, Ralph Waldo Emerson, (Boston: J. Munroe: 1844).

"The Secret Mind, the Silken Nerve": *Judith, Esther and Other Poems*, Maria Gowen Brooks, (Boston: Cummings & Hilliard, 1820). Also, "Be faithful   Go" ends Zbigniew Herbert's "The Envoy of Mr. Cogito"; the Carpenters and Valles both translate it the same way.

"*In Love's Soft Surgery Skill'd*": Section LX, *Zóphiël: or the Bride of Seven*, Maria Gowen Brooks, (London: RJ Kennett, 1833).

"Plate Tectonics": *Paradiso*, Canto XXII, Dante Alighieri, *The Divine Comedy*, (trans. Charles Eliot Norton (Chicago: Encyclopedia Britannica: 1955). Dante says, "then I turned back my eyes to the beautiful eyes."

"Past All Accident": "The Ivy Crown," *Journey to Love*, William Carlos Williams, (NY: Random House, 1955).

Acknowledgments

I am grateful to the editors of the following magazines
in which some of these poems first appeared:

*Alligator Juniper; American Literary Review; American Poetry Review;
Boulevard; Forklift, Ohio; Harvard Review; The Laurel Review;
Marlboro Review; Narrative; New England Review; Pleiades;
Shenandoah; Slate; Sou'wester; Studio* (Canada)*; Superstition Review;
Threepenny Review; Witness;* and *The Yale Review.*

"'Tis Often Thus with Spirits" was reprinted on Verse Daily,
August 6, 2006.

"Parable" was written for Arielle Greenberg and Rachel Zucker's blog
Starting Today: Poems for Obama's First 100 Days, and reprinted in the
anthology of the same title (University of Iowa Press, 2010).

For their astute and generous thoughts as this book progressed, I am
grateful to Jim Longenbach, Kevin Prufer, Matt Hart, Ilya Kaminsky,
Chris Nealon, Eric Pankey, and Martha Rhodes. I'm grateful as well
to Richard Abate, Scott Baxter, Victoria McCoy, and everyone at
Barrow Street, especially Peter Covino, Talvikki Ansel, and
Rob Drummond.

Also, my thanks to the Arizona Commission on the Arts,
Arizona State University, the Bread Loaf Writers' Conference, and
the Ucross Foundation for their support.

Many of the poems here are dedicated to Jean Ball and Jen King,
and to Jerry Ball, in memory.

Mike, Oscar, Celia, and Ted: thank you, too. And love—

This book is for Louise.

Sally Ball is also the author of *Annus Mirabilis* (Barrow Street Press Poetry Prize, 2005). She is an associate director of Four Way Books, and she teaches in the MFA program at Arizona State University in Tempe.

Barrow Street Poetry

Wreck Me
Sally Ball (2013)

Blight, Blight, Blight, Ray of Hope
Frank Montesonti (2012)

Self-evident
Scott Hightower (2012)

Emblem
Richard Hoffman (2011)

Mechanical Fireflies
Doug Ramspeck (2011)

Warranty in Zulu
Matthew Gavin Frank (2010)

Heterotopia
Lesley Wheeler (2010)

This Noisy Egg
Nicole Walker (2010)

Black Leapt In
Chris Forhan (2009)

Boy with Flowers
Ely Shipley (2008)

Gold Star Road
Richard Hoffman (2007)

Hidden Sequel
Stan Sanvel Rubin (2006)